WHAT and HOW

Tools of the trade for drummers

By Richard Wilson

Contents.

About the Author

Richard is one of the UK's leading private drum teachers and also the owner of RAW Studios, the leading private music tuition studio in the North of England.

Richard has been playing drums since the age of 9 and has played many gigs, from rock and pop to funk and jazz. He also spent many years playing in some of the UK's leading drums corps and marching bands, allowing him to perfect his rudimental skills and techniques.

Richard has studied the art of playing drums throughout his career with many teachers, giving him a chance to learn from them and then putting this into his own distinct way of teaching.

Richard's outlook towards drumming changed in the early 2000s when he went to have a lesson with master teacher and drummer Dom Famularo. Richard's whole approach to playing and thinking about drums was changed from that moment onwards.

Without the mentorship and guidance from Dom, none of the success Richard has achieved would have been possible, and for that, Richard is eternally grateful to Dom.

Most of the content from this book is Richard's take on what he has been taught by Dom; he has taken his own knowledge and put that together with the knowledge gained from studying with Dom to create a one-stop shop for all things related to **HOW** to play and approach playing the drums.

What is "What and How" ?

Imagine you have a beautiful piece of RAW Steak that you are about to prepare for your evening meal. You have all the ingredients to make a perfect meal, but without the knowledge of how to get the most from the ingredients it will never turn out the way you want it.

Think of your drumming as that piece of RAW Steak.

It is really easy for us all, with the resources w+e have nowadays, to go online and look at our favourite drummers and try and copy the Grooves and Fills that you see **(THE WHAT),** but without the knowledge and understanding to make these things work **(THE HOW)** we will never achieve our goals and play like our influences and idols.

This book is going to plant seeds in your mind and get you to think about HOW you should approach different things as you go about your everyday life as a drummer, whether that's as a Pro or a complete novice. Of course, if you are a complete beginner, then we will need to seek out a great teacher to show you the concepts and ideas discussed in this book.

Here is a little something taught to me many, many years ago:

Technique is ....NOT MESSING WITH NATURE

If something naturally wants to happen then let it !!!!

The Tools of the Trade.

As a modern 21st century drummer, we all have so many tools and techniques at our disposal that allow us to gain massive facility on the drum kit due to new media like the Internet, YouTube, Facebook, and online lessons offered by teachers around the world.

All this new technology is of no use to any drummer unless you can work out how to get the patterns from your head, through your hands and onto the drums.

This means picking the correct Tool for the job.

Imagine you are having a new kitchen fitted in your home, you have spent weeks detailing all the specifications of what you would like, the units are delivered ready for the team to come in and do the installation, and the excitement is now at a high and then the fitter arrives as arranged, and he has only got one hammer and no other tools.

Would you let this workman loose on your house and your new kitchen? I very much doubt it!!

Most of the drummers I come across in my teaching studio in the UK and my online students around the world try and play everything they attempt using one tool (The same technique for everything) and force things to happen without looking in their toolbox for the correct tool for the job.

The following book will give you an insight into the tools that are available for use as a drummer.

If you have been playing for a while, you may know some of this, but it never harms to go back to basics and correct any Habits you may have unknowingly created.

Q. How many of you would pass your driving test today?

A. I suspect a lot would fail based on bad habits that have formed over the years.

Chapter 1 - Grip

This chapter will give you the details you need about all the tools available to you as a modern-day drummer from a hand Technique point of view.

Remember good hand technique is a tool to enable you to play in a more efficient way and to avoid injury, something which I see sadly too much with new students.

Think of technique very much like a lawn mower. Nobody ever bought a lawn mower because they wanted one. They bought one because they wanted to mow the lawn.

Technique is very much the same. It is there to enable you to achieve what you want to on the drum kit.

Matched Grip

Matched grip is when we play with both our hands in the same position i.e. matched.

Within matched grip, we have 3 different options available to get different tones and dynamics.

These are called German Grip, French Grip, American Grip.

German Grip

German grip is from the matched grip position and with the palms of the hands pointing downwards towards the floor.

Imagine trying to play around a barrel. (remember to keep your arms and elbows relaxed and not sticking out).

The grip uses the most muscles of any of the grips discussed in this chapter, hence giving more volume and a very solid sound.

French Grip

French Grip, often referred to as French Timpani grip, is when we bring our hands together with the thumbs on top of the sticks parallel to each other.

The grip uses the Least muscles of any of any of the grips discussed in this chapter, hence giving less volume and a lighter touch on the drum.

American Grip

American falls in between German and French grips, so if German grip is palms down and french grip is thumbs up, then anything in between these two positions will fall into American grip.

This grip uses more muscles than French grip and fewer muscles than German grip hence giving you a dynamic range and tone in between these other two positions.

Example Exercise 1

To test out the different tones you can get from changing between these grips, Hold the stick loosely and play single-stroke 16th notes on a Pad or Snare drum.

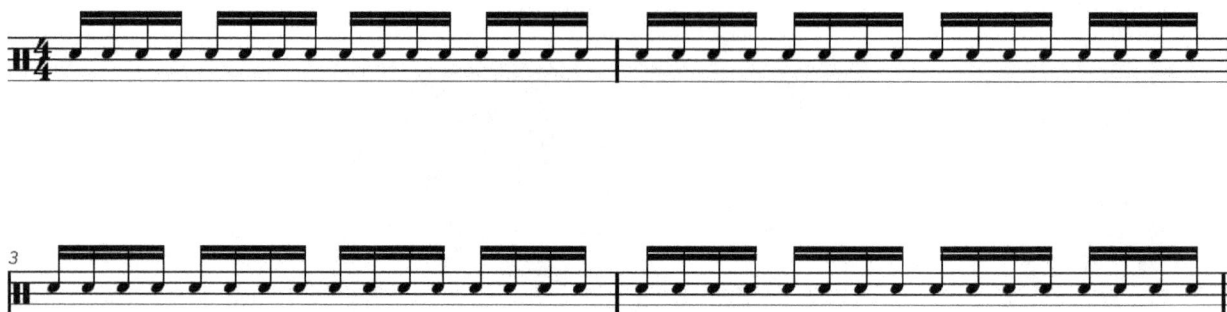

Start Palms down in German and play one bar of 16th notes.

Without stopping, move into American grip (you will start to hear a lighter, less dense tone from the pad or drum).

Again, without stopping, move in French grip (This time, you will hear a significant difference in tone and volume from the previous grips).

If you do not hear the changes, immediately try this exercise again, making sure you are not gripping the stick too tightly and choking the sound.

* Testing if you are choking the sticks and drums*

Take your sticks, grip them tightly, and hit them together.

With the stick gripped in this way, what you will hear is a dull, choked sound with no resonance at all.

Now, take the same sticks, grip them loosely and hit them together again. This time, you should hear the resonance of the wood sing out.

If you play with the sticks choked, then all your drums are going to sound choked, and you will be working way too hard for too few results.

NB: Knocking the sticks together in this way is also a good way to see if your sticks are starting to break or crack from the inside.

If you play with uneven sticks, you will get an uneven sound, that's just a fact!!!!!!!!!

Remember, when working on your hands and playing, in general, to keep your thumbs on the stick.

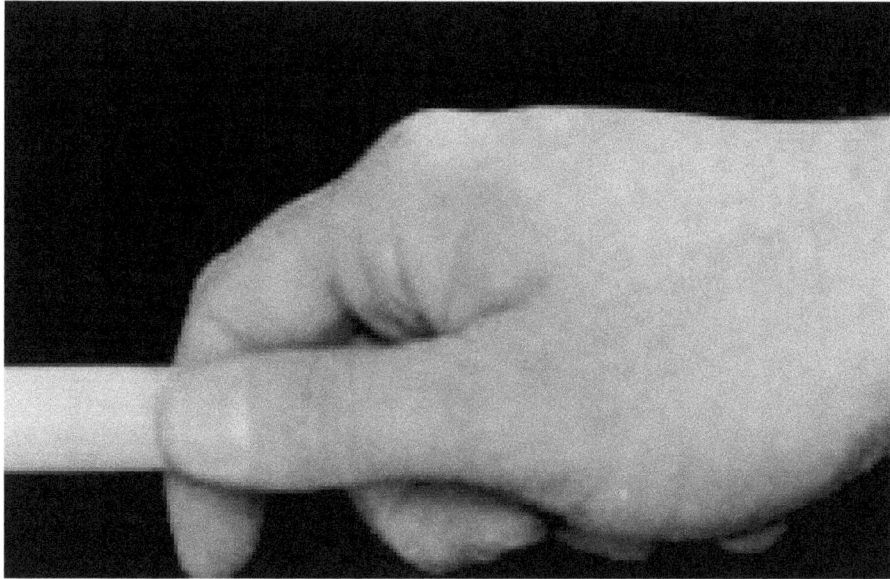

The thumb is the part of the grip that helps to keep control and keeps the stick going straight up and down. Without the thumb in the correct position, the stick can fall into the gap in your hand. All it takes is one mistimed hit of a cymbal or to catch a rim during a fill and control has gone.

Once this happens, you lose full control, and the stick ends up with the thumb below it

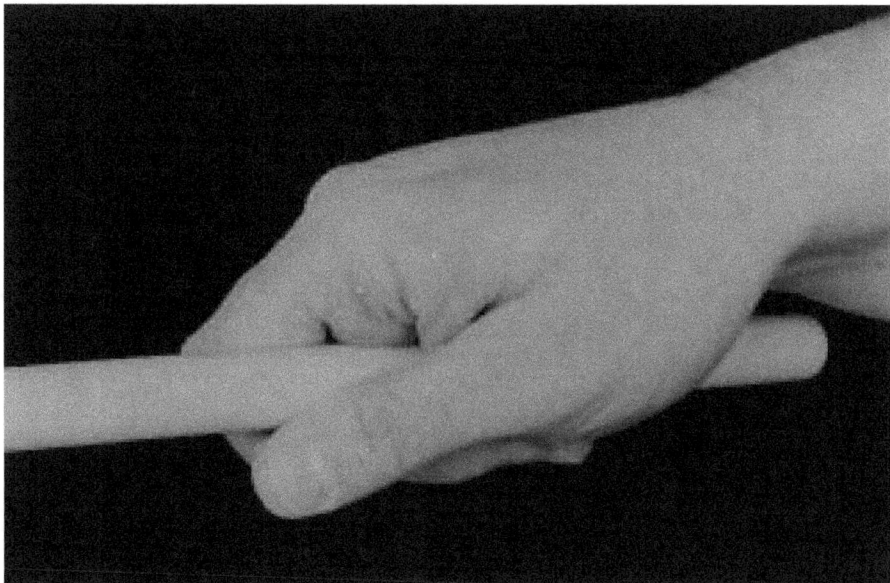

or even worse in a fist

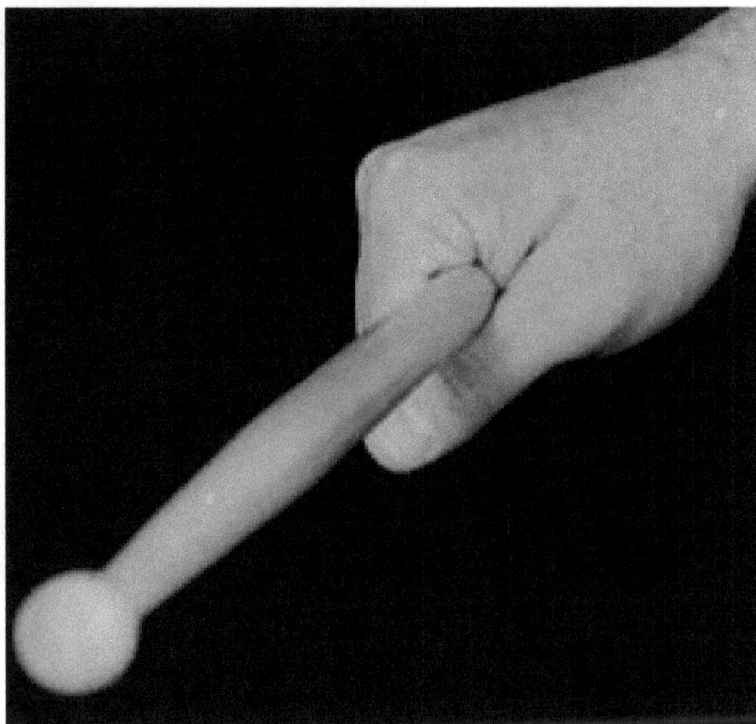

In my own teaching, I find a vast majority of the time the thumb is the main reason why students don't achieve what they want from their hands.

The main position I see is with the thumb slightly too low on the stick.

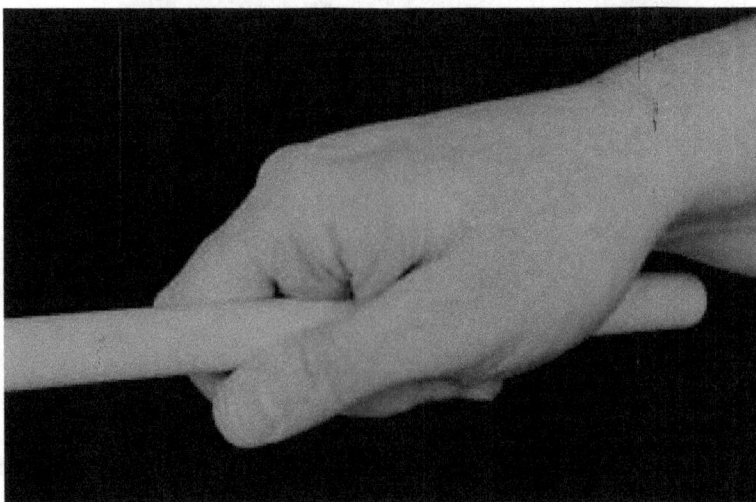

This grip causes the stick to be able to fall into the gap and no longer go up and down but around in a circular motion, hence making the strokes from hand to hand very uneven.

This tends to be mainly on the student's weaker side, so left if you are a right-handed player.

The next time you practice, try paying real attention to where your thumb is in relation to your stick. I feel sure it will make a difference to your control with a little work.

Chapter 2 - Stick Heights Controlling Volume or Dynamics

Within our hand technique, we have looked at ways to control the tone and density of the sound we are producing.

Now, let's look at ways to change the volume or dynamics of our playing.

*Many people and lots of my students from around the world, when they come to me, think that to play louder, you need to hit the drums harder. **This is simply not true.***

Just as we controlled the tone and density of the notes we play by adjusting our grip we control the volume or dynamics by controlling the height of each stroke.

We have three options for controlling the height.

Full Stroke Half Stroke Low Stroke

Below are some images of the three strokes. Notice the relation between them.

Full Stroke.

The Full Stroke is at an almost 90-degree angle to the surface you are striking.

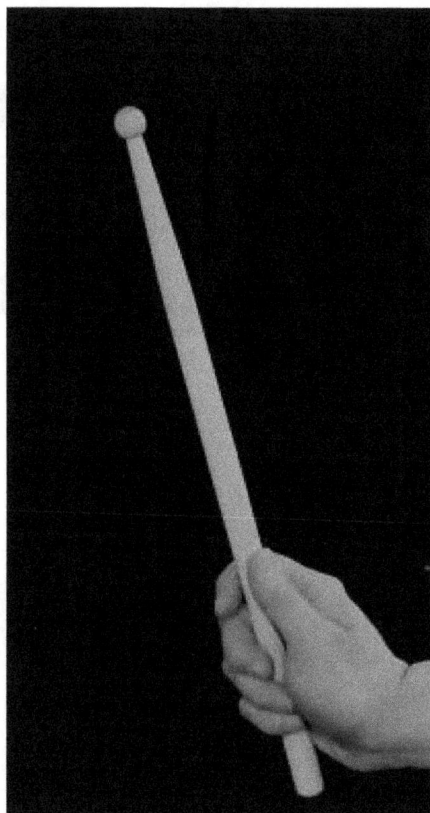

Half Stroke.

The Half Stroke is at a 45-degree angle to the surface you are striking.

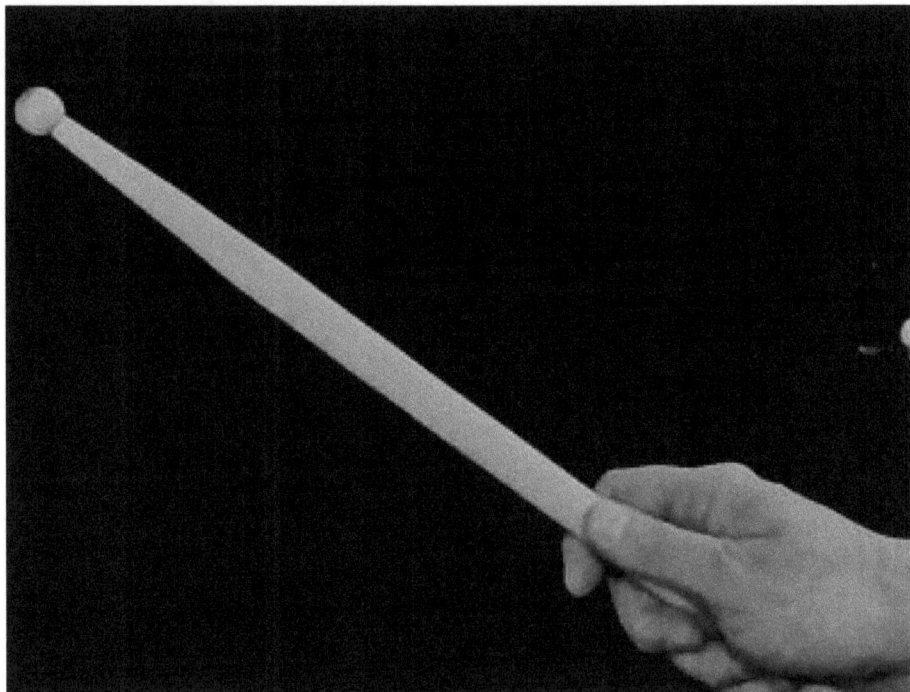

Low Stroke.

The low stroke is almost parallel to the surface you are striking.

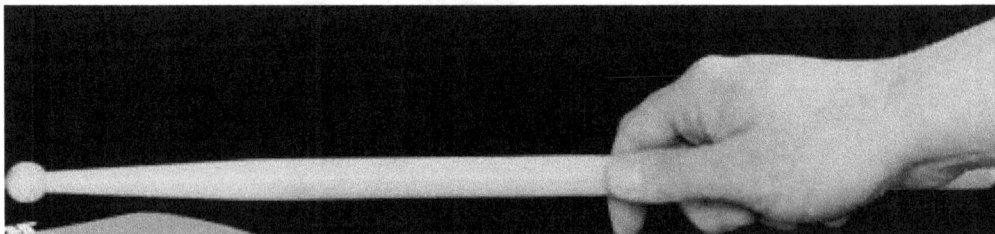

Example exercise 2

Grip the stick loosely and play single-stroke 16th notes as we did in exercise 1

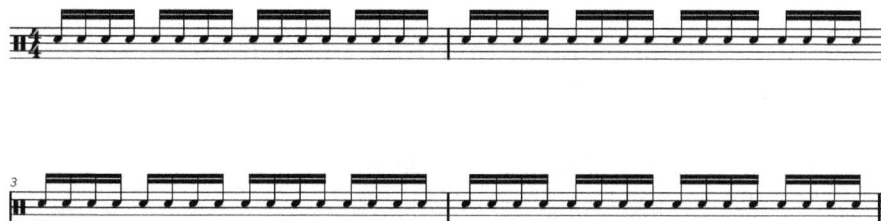

Start in the full-stroke position and play 4 bars (paying attention to the sound). Then, move to the half-stroke position without stopping (again, listen to the sound). Finally, move to the low stroke position.

What you should hear without changing anything else in your technique, only the height is a dramatic change in the volume of your single strokes.

Repeat this a few times, and remember not to change anything about your technique. Keep it loose and let the sticks do the work.

Chapter 3 - Strokes

Free Stroke

(You can try this out in chapter 3 using the WHAT and HOW chart; the free stroke falls into the movement category using the Wrist.)

When thinking about the free stroke, imagine the motion you use when bouncing a ball; you push the ball down, and it comes back. This is the same motion you use when playing the free stroke.

Many people stop the stick at the bottom of the stroke and then pull the stick back up. This is way too much effort for no results.

If you think about the actions you need to take to stop the stick and bring it back up, you will be surprised how many there are:

Example:

This is an example of what you need to do to stop the stick and then pull it back up.

Starting at the full stroke position. Push the stick = 1 Action

Stop the Stick = 2 Actions Squeeze the Stick = 3 Actions Pull the stick = 4 Actions

Remember, you have only hit the drum once so far and used 4 actions.

Here is an example of the same thing using the free stroke, Starting at the full stroke position.

*Push the stick and let it come back into your hand. Once you get this going = **1 Action job Done!!!!!!!***

With the first example, to play a bar of 16th notes, you will need 4 actions per note, giving you a total of 64 actions to achieve one bar of music. Multiply this by an entire piece of music, and you can see you are working way too hard.

The Key to this is to let the Sticks and Drums do the work so you don't have to.

Moeller.

The Moeller technique is a technique developed by legendary teacher Sanford Moeller.

The technique is based around a whipping motion of the stick towards the drum Head, much the same as the motion you would use to crack a whip, remembering to keep the stick loose.

(You can try this out in chapter 6 using the WHAT and HOW chart; the Moeller falls into the Movement category using the Arm)

The way to start with the Moeller technique is to imagine that the tip of the stick weighs a thousand pounds. When you lift the stick from the drum or pad, the back or butt end of the stick will come up first, leaving the tip resting down.

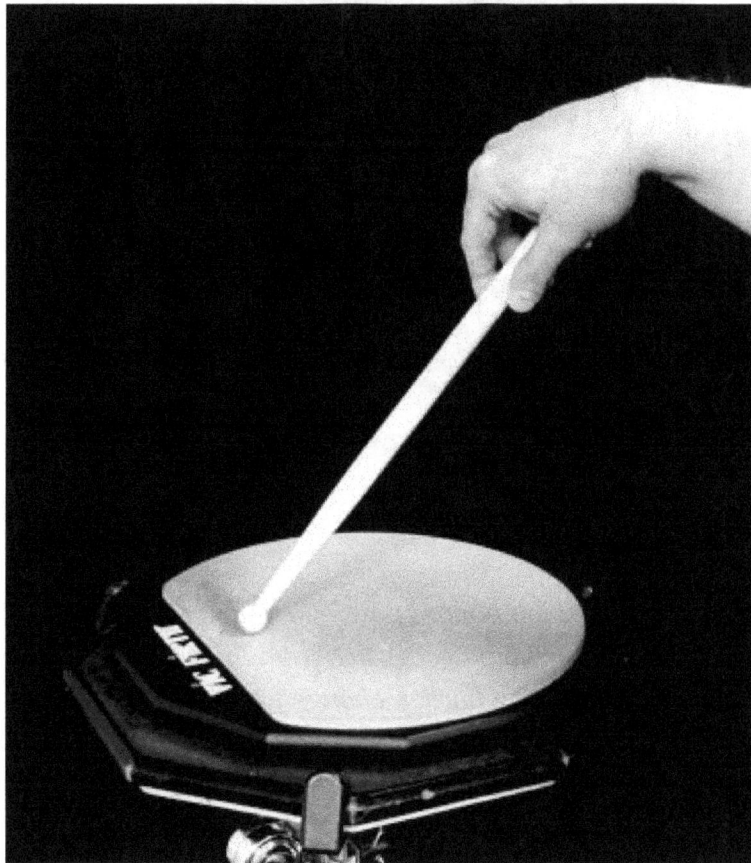

The start position of the Moeller very much differs from the start position of the free stroke.

In the Free Stroke, the tip of the stick is the first part to be raised from the head,

In the Moeller, it is the last part to leave and almost be dragged upwards into the whip position.

The Moeller technique is used to give power and speed from the arm.

Power

The Moeller can be used to develop more power in your playing due to it employing the bigger muscles in your arm and the force that can be generated from the whipping motion. If you want a bigger backbeat in a song, then rather than hitting harder, change to the Moeller, and it will do the job for you. Always be aware that the Moeller stroke should not be forced. By its very nature, the technique itself will give you the power you need.

Speed

When we start to play faster, most of the time, we need to play with a lower stroke. This is due to the time it takes to travel from stroke height to the drum or pad if we try and play fast from a full stroke position, it simply takes too long to get to the drum or pad.

Enabling the Moeller technique allows you to make the stroke height bigger again and hence gives you more speed. Also, by using the bounce from the whip, you effectively get several notes for free.

Example exercise

Play some hand-to-hand triplets - RLR LRL RLR LRL (OR REVERSED IF YOU ARE LEFT HANDED)

Use the Free Stroke on the beat, so counts 1 2 3 and 4

Measure the tempo with a Metronome or click and record this down.

NEXT

*Replace the free strokes on the beat with a Moeller Whip (**Whip** and er, **Whip** and er, **Whip** and er, **Whip** and er,). Again, measure the tempo with a click.*

It will eventually be faster.

If you don't get it the first time, then keep practising and make sure the whipping motion is correct and **NOT FORCED.**

With only this simple exercise, you should already be able to see that changing the way you play depending on the situation you are in will offer you a completely different sound and approach to the drum kit, and we are only just starting to scratch the surface.

Chapter 4 - Practice log

PRACTICE TIP: *practice with a click and record the exercise you are working on and your speed in a practice log. This way, you can physically see progress on paper when you look back. Also, it is a good guide to show your teacher so he or she can see where you are getting stuck, what exercises you are finding easy, and what exercises you are finding challenging. This is a quicker route to getting any issues with your hands sorted out quickly.*

This can be very inspiring if you get stuck in a rut with an exercise.

Many of my own students over the years have found massive benefits from keeping an updated practice log. In fact many students attend lessons with exercise books full of detailed recordings of what they have been working on in their own practice time away from lessons.

EXAMPLE OF A SIMPLE PRACTICE LOG TEMPLATE.

PRACTICE TIP: *When you practice anything to do with your playing, don't try and get perfection the first time. The idea of practice is that you work on something that you can't play. At first, this is, of course, going to sound terrible, but this is the point of practice.*

*If every time you practice, you play everything the first time. This means you are only practising things you already know how to play and **NOT** pushing yourself enough.*

Next time you sit down at your kit in the practice room, think about this statement.

Chapter 5 - The tools in more detail.

The following chart will help you to look at **HOW** to achieve the motion or sound you want to play in your everyday drumming situations.

WHAT and HOW !!!

GRIP	Movement
German	Arm
French	Wrist
American	Fingers

Stick Height	Fulcrum
Full	Very loose
Half	Loose
Low	Slight pinch

Explanation of WHAT and HOW chart

Grip - *The Section of the chart refers to the way you play within matched grip. See Chapter One for a detailed explanation of the grips available to you.*

Stick Height - *This section of the chart explains the way we can gain more control and dynamics by simply changing the height in which you strike the head from*

There is no set rule to these heights, but make sure to get them relevant to each other.

EG, If the height of your full stroke is 15", then make your half 10" and low 5"

These are just a guide, but the main point is that you don't have a full stroke of 15", Half at 12" and then low at 3"

Movement - *This section of the chart gives you the options with your motion.*

Arm - This relates to the Moeller technique.

Wrist - This relates to the Free Stroke and a wrist motion. Fingers - This relates to the finger technique.

Fulcrum - *This section of the chart looks at the way you grip the stick to enable full control and range of motion.*

Very Loose - This is placing the stick in the hand and leaving it very loose so the stick can rebound back fully with no resistance.

Loose - Rather than very loose, this gives you a little more control over your strokes.

Slight pinch - This is when we need a little more control. For example, when playing a low stroke at high speed, we will need to have a slight pinch on the stick to enable us to get the control we need.

*NOTE: THE SLIGHT PINCH IS EXACTLY THAT: A **SLIGHT PINCH.** THIS IS STILL GOING TO FEEL LOOSE IF YOU ARE USED TO GRIPPING TIGHTLY*

Chapter 6 - Using the WHAT and HOW chart.

Examples of how to plot your approach to an exercise or groove

Accent and Ghost notes.

R - Accent right hand L - Accent left hand

r - Ghost note right-hand l - Ghost note left-handed

R l R l RlRl LrLr Lr Lr

Most drummers would try and play this using the same grip, motion, Stick height and fulcrum, but this is not going to work in an efficient way.

Here is the way that I would suggest you approach this.

For the accents

Choose your grip. Any of them will work for this. I would be in German or American for this.

The Stick height for the accent needs to be full or half, depending on the volume of accent you require.

The motion should be arm or wrist again, depending again on the volume of the accent.

Big full accents = German, Full, Arm, Very loose Small, more controlled accents - American, Half, Wrist, Loose.

For the Ghost notes.

The ghost notes need to be played with much control, so I would suggest plotting the following on the chart.

American, Low, Wrist, Slight pinch

You will need the slight pinch to enable you to have the control you need to play the stroke at a low height.

*NOTE: THE SLIGHT PINCH IS EXACTLY THAT: A **SLIGHT PINCH**. THIS IS STILL GOING TO FEEL LOOSE IF YOU ARE USED TO GRIPPING TIGHTLY*

After reading this, get out your pad and sticks, pay real attention to the exercise above, and see if you can feel and hear the difference.

Another way to practice this is with your eyes closed. As we take away one sense the others become heightened. Using this method makes you hear the difference between your accents and ghost notes.

Note: Really focus on the evenness and quality of your ghost notes.

Don't rush this. Take your time. After all, you are changing the way you approach your playing. This will take time.

REMEMBER, LEARNING ANYTHING IS A MARATHON, NOT A SPRINT, DON'T RUSH IT.

Chapter 7 - Real World Scenarios

In this chapter, let's look at a very basic groove that you will all probably know already (if you are a pro, don't be scared to go back to basics every so often. This really helps).

The Groove we are going to use is a very basic 8th-note rock groove.

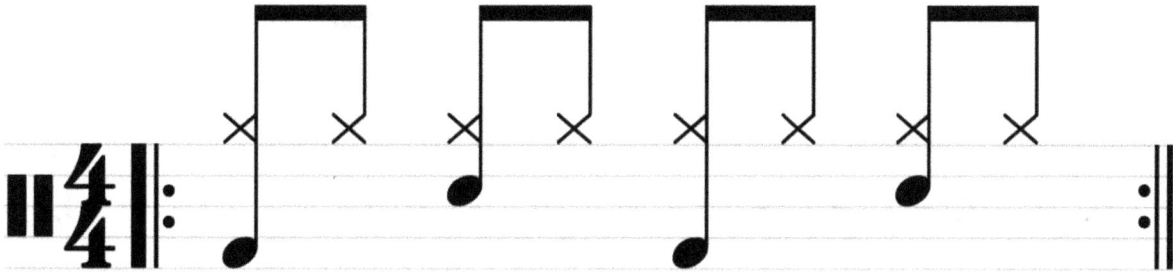

Once we have this groove working, let's look at a few scenarios you may find yourself in needing to play with this groove.

Scenario 1.

Imagine you have been called to a gig, and the first song has this groove. You approach it in your normal way (have a think about what this means to you). The bandleader stops the song and says to you, that's nice, but can we have a little more snare but keep the Hi Hat low.

Q. What are you going to do?

A. Play the Hi hat with low strokes, and from an American position, push the arm forward to leave a space for the Snare hand.

Play the snare with a full stroke from the German position, either using the free stroke or the Moeller, depending on how big you want the backbeat.

Scenario 2.

You are now playing the same groove in another song when, once again, you are stopped because all the groove is too loud and not sitting well with the band.

Q. What are you going to do?

A. Move your hands to a low or half stroke position using the Wrist (Free Stroke and don't apply any Moeller to this at all).

*This may sound very, very easy, and in a way, it really is, it's just that most drummers don't pay any attention to the **HOW** they are playing. They just focus on the **WHAT** they are playing.*

*Again, think of the steak. In both scenarios, you have had the perfect piece of RAW steak and ruined it by not paying attention to **HOW** to cook it.*

These few little changes to your approach will make a really big difference, and the best part is you don't need to try any harder as the new positions and motions will make the changes for you, making you a more rounded player and ready for any situation.

Lets now have a look at some fill ideas and the motions you could use to get more facility on the drum kit.

The first fill is a simple Paradiddle.

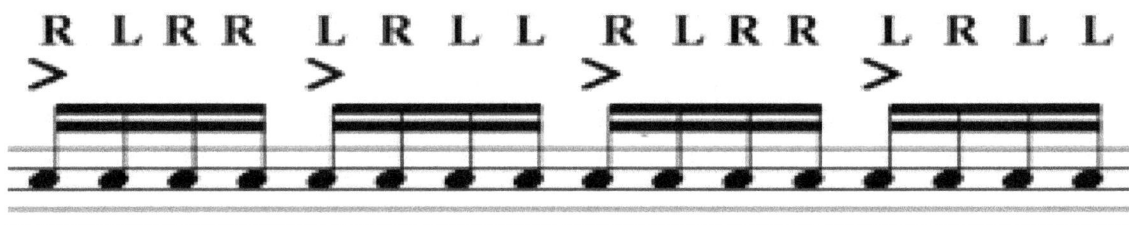

Play the accents on Tom 1 and the rest on the snare using the following grip and motions.

American Grip / Freestroke / Half Height

This will work to a certain point, but as you get more comfortable with it and speed starts to increase, you will find yourself having to work hard to get this flow.

Now, lets think about the HOW in this situation.

Using the free stroke in the first example leaves us with a challenge at speed. Allow me to explain this in more detail.

In getting from the Snare to Tom 1 at speed, we have to lift the stick to gain the height needed to play the Tom and also push forward so we can reach the centre of the drum. If we don't lift the stick then we end up playing a full-height stroke on the snare and somewhere between half and low on the tom, thus giving us an uneven fill.

Try this out slowly and see that the snare and tom are now being played from different heights.

Q. How we get around the issue?

A. We use the Moeller. Once you have got to grips with the Moeller, either from chapter 1 in this book or from your teacher, you will see that playing a Moeller stroke from the Snare allows you to just push forward a little and still get that nice big sound we are looking for to even out your fill.

Try this exercise

Play a Moeller stroke on the snare and then finish back in the start position (the Serpents head).

Now, try playing a stroke on every drum you have on your kit and how little you have to move to achieve this. If you are unsure of this, run the same exercise without the Moeller, so play each drum and stop the stick once it has struck the head.

See the Difference?

*This is the power of **HOW** and how we need to use this to our advantage.*

Another way to use the Moeller to your advantage when playing paradiddles is to think about it in a completely different way. Don't think about the 8th or 16th note or the sticking pattern, but work on it in the following way.

Play a Moeller triplet with your leading hand.

3

D = Down

T = Tap

U - UP

D   T   U

    Do this at a relatively slow speed, and once you get this, even try adding a ghost note with your other hand in between the DOWN and the TAP.

1.   *and*   *er*

(ghost)

Downstroke.   *Tap.*   *Upstroke*

    Now you have a very lumpy Paradiddle.

    With this in mind, now try to even this out so you can play a nice-sounding paradiddle. You will need to just hang back a little bit on with the TAP and UPSTROKE.

    Once this is even repeat these steps leading with your other hand. You will soon find your Paradiddles flow more, and as we are already using the Moeller, moving them around the kit and gaining speed will become very easy.

This book is only just scratching the surface of the hand techniques available to us as drummers, it is designed to be a starting point to make you more efficient when playing in any given situation.

I would suggest searching out a proven tutor and asking them about the motions and mechanics of your playing, and this includes seasoned professional players. I had been playing for 20 years before I met my good friend, mentor, and master teacher, Mr Dom Famularo. Dom showed me all of these techniques in great detail, and without this time with Dom I would not be the player and teacher I am today.

*Please try out the ideas in this book and remember to always think about the **HOW** as well as the* **WHAT!!!!**

REMEMBER TO WORK ON EXERCISES SLOWLY TO START WITH AND THEN SPEED THEM UP.

Also, remember technique is a means to an end, something I use with all my students, and something I mentioned in chapter one is:

Technique is like a lawn mower. Nobody ever bought a lawn mower to just have a lawn mower. They bought one to mow the lawn.

Technique is the same. It is there to make our facility on the drums better to better serve the music we are playing.

BUT ABOVE ALL ELSE PLEASE REMEMBER TO HAVE FUN WHILE PLAYING.

Drums and music, in general, are some of the most creative pursuits we have available to us.

Good Luck!

Notes: